To:

From:

Happy Reading!

CHRONICLES OF CORYN:

ADVENTURES IN SAINT KITTS AND NEVIS

Coryn ♡

Written by: Coryn Anaya Clarke

Illustrated by: Sameer Kassar

© 2021 Coryn Anaya Clarke

All rights reserved. No portion of this book may be reproduced in any form or by any means, electronic or mechanical, including photocopying and recording, or by any information
storage or retrieval system without the written permission of the author.

ISBN: 9798549328334

Published by Caribbean Unicorn Publications

Illustrations by Sameer Kassar

This book is for:

My great-granny Leontine Clarke, Mama Jenn and Papito.

I love you, I miss you and I can't wait to see you again.

Hello friends! I am excited and so very happy. Do you know why?

I'm vacationing in Saint Kitts and Nevis! We'll be here for ten days.

I was born in Trinidad and Tobago, my mummy too, but my daddy was born in Saint Kitts and Nevis.

I've been here twice before to visit my relatives.

Mama Jenn, Papito, and Uncle Rae live in Saint Kitts.
My great-granny, aunty Joya, Aunty Joyce, aunty Nola and Uncle Mackie are just some of my relatives who live on Nevis.

I'm really excited to spend time with them.

My daddy said, now that I'm a bit older, I can finally get the true tourist experience.

A tourist is someone who leaves their country to visit another country.

I left Trinidad to visit Saint Kitts and Nevis, so I'm a tourist.

I can't wait to explore.

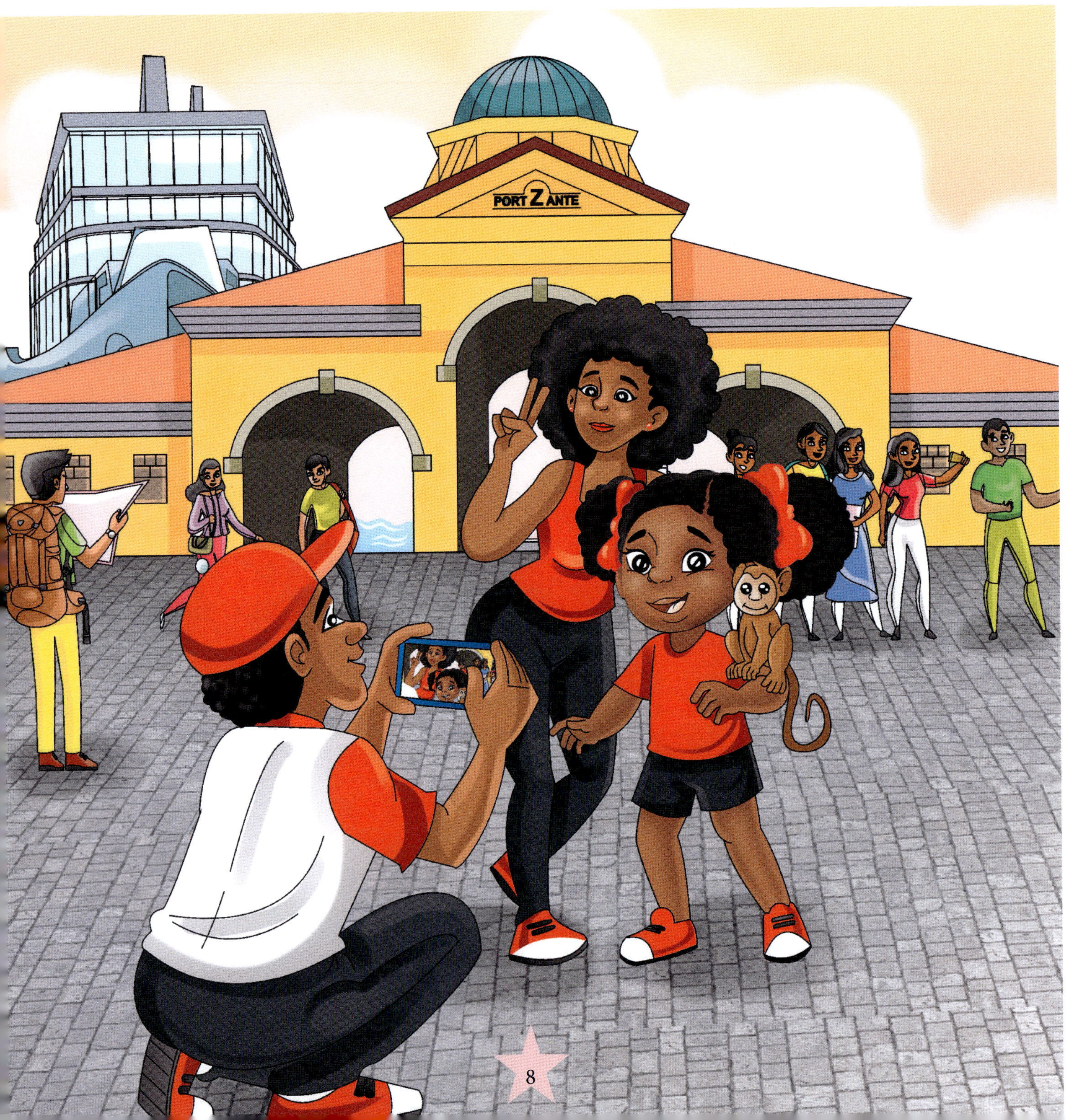
PORT Z ANTE

DAY 1: PORT ZANTE

Today we went to Port Zante, that's where all the huge ships dock.

When the ships come to Saint Kitts, tourists visit all the shops around Port Zante to purchase souvenirs.

A souvenir is something you buy to help you remember the trip.

My daddy said Port Zante is important to Saint Kitts and Nevis because a lot of the money needed to build schools and create jobs come from the cruise tourists who visit the island.

Port Zante is a fun place to explore.

We saw men walking around with monkeys dressed in the cutest little outfits.

Monkeys wearing clothes, isn't that crazy?

Daddy said tourists like to hold and pet them and even take pictures with them.

I'm a tourist, so I did it too.

QUICK FACT: Port Zante was first opened in 2005.

10

DAY 2: THE SAINT KITTS SCENIC RAILWAY

Today we rode on a train.

At first, I was scared because I had never been on a train before, but this train ride was lots of fun.

We got yummy treats and refreshing juices, but my favourite part was the music.

The tour operators taught us songs and told us stories about Saint Kitts and Nevis.

I learned that the St Kitts Scenic Railway is one of the islands main tourist attractions.

You remember what a tourist is, don't you?

The tour guide said a long time ago, the train was used to transport sugar cane from the plantations to the mills.

At the mills, the sugar cane was crushed, processed, and made into the sugar that we use to make yummy treats like red velvet cupcakes.

When they stopped making sugar in Saint Kitts and Nevis, the trains were

RE-PUR-POSED. Repurposed!

That means they are now being used for something else, like giving fun tours.

QUICK FACT: The railway in Saint Kitts was built between 1912 and 1926 to transport sugar cane from the plantations to the sugar factory in Basseterre, the capital of Saint Kitts.

13

POINCIANA, THE NATIONAL FLOWER OF SAINT KITTS AND NEVIS

The National Flower of Saint Kitts and Nevis is the Poinciana.

Can you say it with me? Poin-ci-ana. Poinciana!

That's a tricky word to pronounce, but another name for the Poinciana is Flamboyant.

Mummy said that name fits because the tree is big, bright and beautiful. I agree!

The flowers are red with hints of yellow.

The Poinciana tree can grow as tall as forty feet.

That is almost six times taller than my daddy is!

There are many Poinciana trees all around the island.

Looking at them make me feel happy.

QUICK FACT: The Poinciana was named after Monsieur de Pincy, the first French Governor of Saint Kitts.

The Royal Poinciana, the national flower of Saint Kitts and Nevis.

DAY 3: BRIMSTONE HILL

Brimstone Hill is a huge fortress at the very top of a huge hill in Saint Kitts.

I was very happy we didn't have to walk all the way to the top.

From the top of the hill, we could see the ocean and the tip of a tiny island that's not too far away.

That island is Saint Eustatius. Papito promised to take me there one day.

I enjoyed our trip to Brimstone Hill very much.

Mummy said the fortress was built by our AN-CES-TORS many, many years ago.

I can't wait to learn more about Brimstone Hill

and the other fun places in Saint Kitts and Nevis.

Learning is fun.

QUICK FACT: Brimstone Hill was built by African slaves. It was first used by the British army in 1690 when a canon was installed to chase away their enemies.

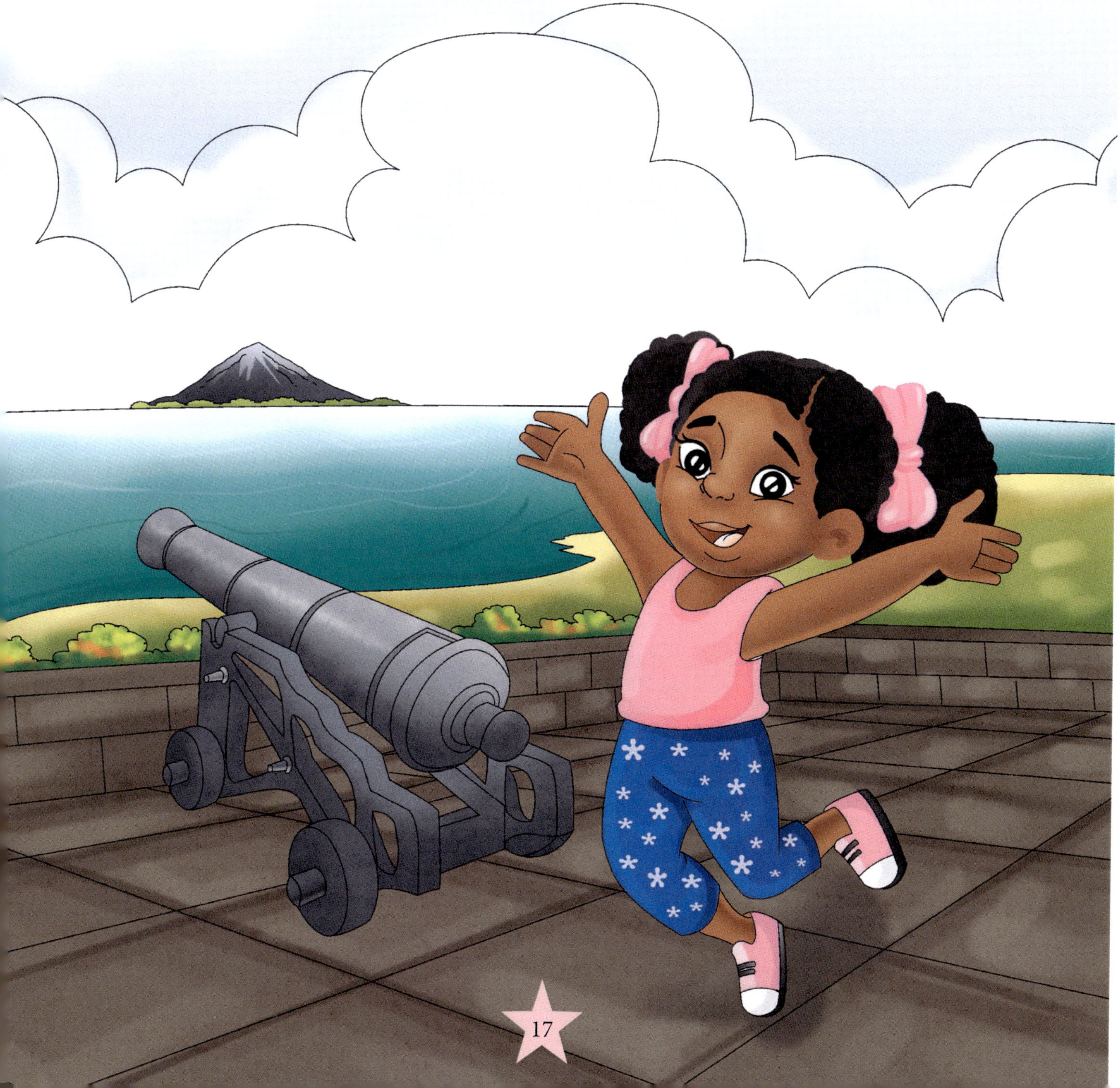

DAY 4: CARIBELLE BATIK

Caribelle Batik is a store in the middle of the Romney Manor Garden in Saint Kitts.

It's one of the prettiest places on the island. There are beautiful flowers and the most HU-MON-GOUS trees I have ever seen! Humongous is just another word for big.

There are many things to see at Caribelle Batik, but my favourite part of that trip was chasing butterflies in the garden.

A tour guide told us that Amerindians lived there a long time ago before Europeans invaded the island. IN-VA-DED means they left their own country and travelled to Saint Kitts without being invited and just took over the areas where the Amerindians lived.

I wouldn't be happy if strange people appeared out of nowhere and took my home away, would you?

We saw drawings on rocks called PE-TRO-GLYPHS, which were made by the Amerindians hundreds of years ago. Mummy said those markings are important because it shows us how they lived.

QUICK FACT: Saint Kitts was the first West Indian island to be colonised by Europeans.

19

PELICAN, THE NATIONAL BIRD OF SAINT KITTS AND NEVIS

The national bird of Saint Kitts and Nevis is the pelican.

These birds love water and can usually be found close to the ocean.

Boobies have a really interesting way of eating.

They dive from high up in the sky and scoop fish up from the sea.

QUICK FACT: The people in Saint Kitts and Nevis call pelicans, boobies.

21

DAY 5: NEVIS, HERE I COME!

Today we're visiting my granny on Nevis! We had to take a ferry to get to her house.

A ferry is a boat that transports people from Saint Kitts to Nevis and then back again.

We have ferries at home too. We use the ferries to travel between Trinidad and Tobago.

When we got to the Basseterre Ferry Terminal in Saint Kitts Daddy bought tickets for us to sail on the Caribe Breeze.

Mummy was afraid that she would fall into the ocean, but I wasn't. The ferry ride was lots of fun.

WELCOME TO BASSETERRE FERRY TERMINAL

ENTRANCE

TICKET BOOTH

We met some really interesting people on the ferry.

Some of them were going to work, some of them were tourists and were going to explore.

I made a list of all the places and people we are going to visit while we are on Nevis.

There is the Nevis Art Gallery, the Hot Springs, the Botanical Gardens,

the beaches, and so much more.

I want to see it all!

QUICK FACT: 11 000 people live on the island of Nevis, which spans 36 square miles.

25

DAY 6: MEET MY GRANNY

My great-grandmother is Leontine Clarke. She is 97 years old.

She is a special lady, and I love her very much.

My granny has the softest skin, the kindest eyes, and she tells the best stories.

I enjoy hearing stories about my daddy as a boy, best of all.

My granny loves music, I do too. We enjoy singing songs together.

What do you love best about your granny?

27

THE NEVIS MANGO FESTIVAL

In Nevis, there are over 40 different types of mangoes to choose from.

Every year they host a mango festival where chefs make yummy mango dishes to compete for the grand prize.

Mama Jenn loves mangoes, that's her favourite fruit.

Do you love mangoes too?

29

DAY 7: THE BOTANICAL GARDENS OF NEVIS

Today we hiked through the Botanical Gardens of Nevis on the Montpelier Estate.

A botanical garden is where plants are grown for scientific research.

Gardeners study the plants and give them the nutrients they need to grow.

Plants need food too, did you know that?

The Nevis Botanical Garden is filled with many different types of plants

and flowers from around the world.

We also saw statues, sculptures and fountains.

It was magical!

QUICK FACT: The Nevis Botanical Gardens covers five acres of land and is close to Mount Nevis.

31

THE ST THOMAS LOWLAND CHURCH

The St. Thomas Anglican Church is the oldest church on the island of Nevis.

It was built in 1643. Daddy helped me to the math, that means it is 378 years old.

Can you believe it?

That's ancient!

What's the oldest building in your country?

33

DAY 8: TO THE BEACH WE GO

There are many beautiful beaches in Saint Kitts and Nevis.

I haven't visited them all, but my favourite so far are Pinney's beach, Oualie and Frigate Bay.

The water is the prettiest shades of blue and green I have ever seen.

These beaches also have the best sand for building sandcastles!

Do you like going to the beach?

Saint Kitts and Nevis have the most amazing beaches in the world!

35

DAY 9: THE FAIRVIEW GREAT HOUSE

Today we toured the Fairview Great House and Gardens.

A tour guide told us it was built around the year 1701 to house French military officers. I couldn't believe it! Built in 1701? That means the house is ancient, but it didn't look that way to me. Mummy explained that the building was restored.

That means parts of it were replaced, rebuilt and repainted.

That's why it looks almost new.

The Fairview Great House is like a museum.

The tour guide showed us ar-ti-facts that were used by people many years ago.

Mummy's favourite part of the tour was the cooking presentation,

but I enjoyed touring the garden best of all.

There were a lot of fruit trees and flowers. We even saw a few cheeky monkeys.

QUICK FACT: The Fairview Great House became a hotel in the 1960's.

37

THE BERKELEY MEMORIAL

The Berkeley Memorial is a tall tower with a clock and a drinking fountain in Basseterre, Saint Kitts.

Daddy said it was built in 1883 to honour the memory of a very important man.

His name was Thomas Hardtman-Berkeley.

He was a legislator and estate owner.

39

DAY 10: INDEPENDENCE SQUARE

Today we went to Independence Square. There's not much to do there but mummy said it's an important part of the country's history.

She said Independence Square is important because it reminds Kittitians and Nevisians of how far they've come.

That means, it reminds them that the country has grown and things are better now than they were a long time ago.

This place was called Pall Mall Square, but the name was changed to Independence Square on September 19, 1983.

Can you guess why?

QUICK FACT: Saint Kitts and Nevis was once the richest British colony.

41

THE TRIP IS ALMOST OVER...

Today is our last day of vacation. Tomorrow we will leave Saint Kitts and return to our home in Trinidad.

I'm happy that I got to visit Mama Jenn, Papito and all my other relatives but I'm really sad that we have to leave. I wish we could stay a bit longer.

My grandparents planned a special family day to make sure that my last day in St Kitts was extra special.

The grownups cooked and chatted while I played with all my cousins who came to visit.

Mummy helped Mama Jenn make goat water, cook-up and conkie, my daddy's favourite meals and dessert. After lunch, we all sat in the living room, and my daddy played the piano while we took turns singing our favourite songs.

Family fun day was the best day ever.

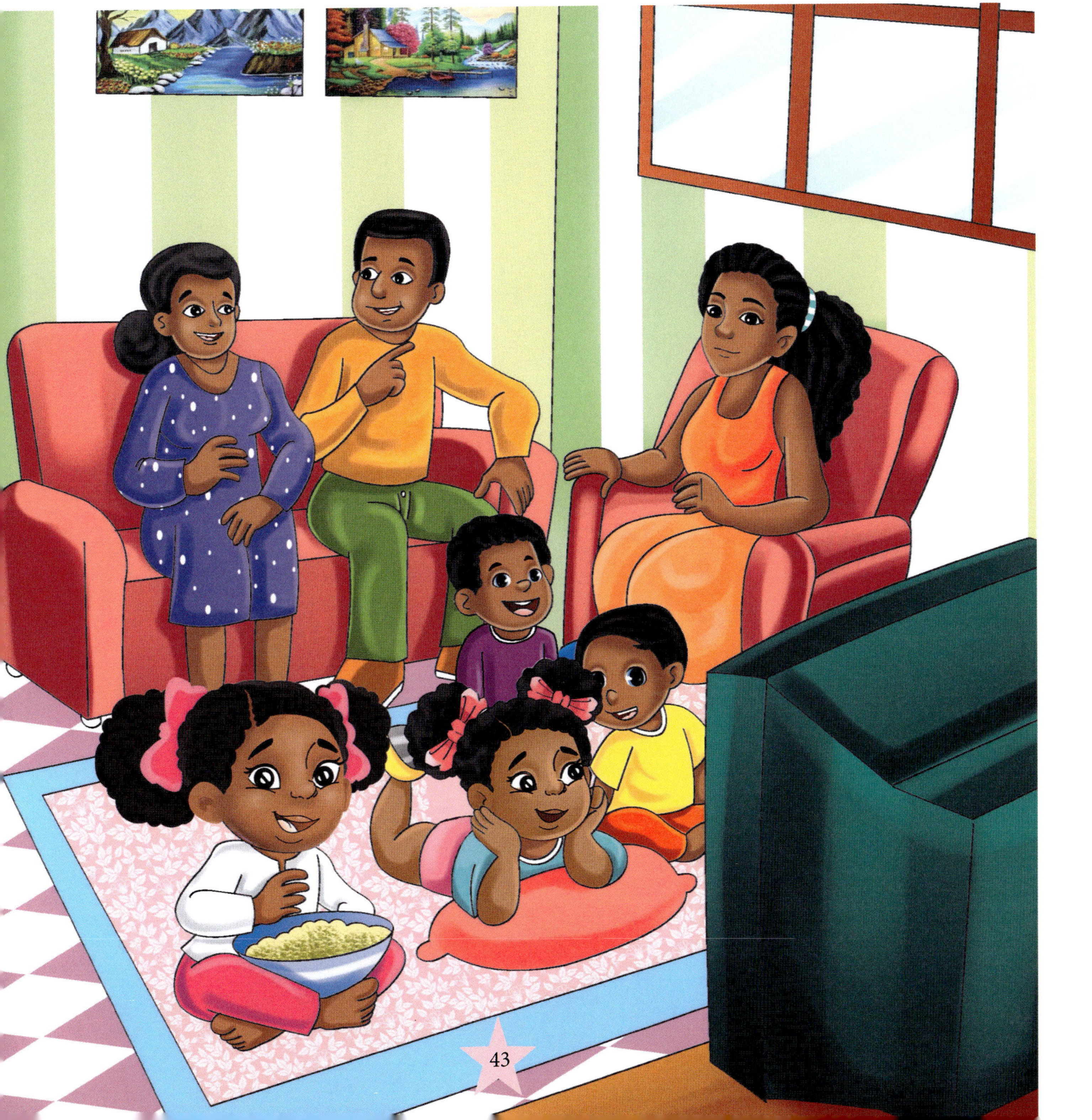

TIME TO GO HOME...

And just like that, the awesome adventure in Saint Kitts and Nevis has come to an end.

I spent time with my family and had a lot of fun exploring and doing touristy things.

We didn't get to see all the sights, but we will next time.

Bye Bye Saint Kitts and Nevis.

45

THE CURRENT LEADERS OF SAINT KITTS AND NEVIS (2015-2025)

Saint Kitts and Nevis are two islands that come together to make one country, just like Trinidad and Tobago.

The leaders of the country are:

Prime Minister Doctor Timothy Harris,

Deputy Prime Minister Shawn Richards and

Premier Mark Brantley.

Together they lead the Team Unity Government.

It is their responsibility to make decision to keep the country safe.

THE LEADERS OF ST. KITTS-NEVIS

Deputy PM Shawn Richards

Prime Minister Dr. Timothy Harris

Premier Mark Brantley

GLOSSARY

PURCHASE: To buy something or to get something by paying for it

SOUVENIR: This is something you buy or make to help you remember a person, place or event

PROCESSED: This is when you add chemicals to a product to preserve it or make it last longer

HUMONGOUS: This is just another word to describe something that really big

INVADED: To take over someone else's space without and invitation or permission

EUROPEANS: People who live in or are from Europe

PETROGLYPHS: These are rock carvings made by people who lived a long time ago

FERRY: A ferry is a boat or ship that is used to transport people from one island to another and back again. Some ferries are used to transport products like food or building materials

COOK-UP: A dish that's made using rice, chicken and lentils or red beans

CONKIE: A popular dessert that's made using sweet potato and coconut

GOAT WATER: Goat water is a type of soup that's made using goat meat, seasonings and vegetables

ANCIENT: Another word for somethings that's really old

ARTIFACTS: These are items that were made a really long time ago that are now an important part of history.

What Are They Saying?

In this book, brilliant young Coryn leads the way on a heart-warming, fact-filled adventure that emphasizes our oneness as Caribbean people. No matter your age, there's much to learn here about our neighbours to the north. To say that this is an impressive work would at this point be redundant. If the future is in the hands of observant, skillful writers and readers like Coryn, there is absolutely no reason to be afraid of it. **-Amanda Choo Quan, Writer**

A great children's book has expansive vocabulary, novel information and isn't a chore for the teacher to read. This book is an absolute delight and simply a must have for any children's school library" **- Kerry-Lee Aranega, Director of Happy Child Nursery School.**

A heartwarming, educational and fun trip with Coryn to St Kitts and Nevis, a Caribbean nation I enjoy visiting too. This book highlights prominent landmarks and teaches children and adults about the history of this beautiful country.
-Yolanda T. Marshall, the author of 'C is for Carnival.'

"Who is this curious, beautiful, bright-eyed, little girl standing before me with such confidence? The first time I met Coryn I was blown away by the way in which, at just 2 years of age, she was able to process and engage in conversation way beyond her years. Watch out world, Chronicles is just the beginning! I am excited to follow Coryn's adventures beyond St, Kitts and Nevis into the future. What a delightful journey...the book and the future!" -
Lisa Wickham, President & CEO Imagine Media International

Made in the USA
Middletown, DE
14 August 2021